A Child's Shor History Book

Black History Month African Study

(In cartoon animal characters)

Fortney

Copyright © 2014 by Albert Fortney Jr. 636518

ISBN: Softcover   978-1-4990-4248-1
       EBook   978-1-4990-4247-4

Rev. date: 07/09/2014

To order additional copies of this book, contact:
Xlibris LLC
1-888-795-4274
www.Xlibris.com
Orders@Xlibris.com

This children's story will end,
being all good like it should
but to adult wrong with mistakes,
said by jungle animals
of people who were not kind,
at the end we'll move on leaving
them behind
and so begins children's Black
History Month of February.
Once upon a time...

in February now begins today
as "History Cleo" the lion strolled whistling through the jungle
on a sweating hot, cloudless noon day,
accidently bumped into his cousin "Kool Leo"
who was humming going about his hazy lazy way.
History Cleo roared, I hope you not in a hurry cous...
I have something very important I'd like to say,
after the greeting of family hugging one another,
it's Black History Month in America honoring their color
Kool Leo roared back, then what happen to it in Africa
it's not celebrated here my courageous lion brother?
History Cleo mildly roared, there were some very bad people
who couldn't picture there being a true black history,
also said they're too good and too great built everything first
and it's bad for business, better they're kept in mystery.

Just then, stepping-out from the jungles dense trees
was big "Jumbo" the Elephant shrilled-out, what's going on
beside you two lions enjoying the breeze?
History Cleo roared, Hello Jumbo you came just in time
this is real serious Jumbo would you please,
elephant scream our meeting now begins spread the News
" black history month" is singing the sad African forgotten Blues.
Jumbo, I cross my heart I ain't lying
it even got cousin Leo boo-hoo crying.

"Goodnite" the Gorilla eating a hand full of bananas for lunch, pushed his way out the thick-brush, was known for one punch would knock your lights out, looking ready to bully a fight...

then grunted to the crowd, two wrongs don't make a right,
being humble has a better power than acting bad with might
stick together, stay strong, stay wise with love, protects;
be yourself don't go for bad, takes more courage and insight.

History Cleo roared, I want every animal here to come together,
we will get a plan to make Black History Month better.
All the different animals gathered around
as the king of the jungle History Cleo
began to really get- down;
here is the story all wondering children will love to hear
from history Cleo the lion, have no fear.

The history of Black people begins with the "Kemet story,"
at that time the greatest nation of power and glory.
The ancient Kemet Nation was the greatest known word for blackness,
living good in learning and building was their practice
until Greek Europeans came and renamed it, their word Egypt why?
It went bad for black Egypt, since changing from Kemet its true,
war became common but changing everything to look like them was new,
 instead of Northeast Africa renamed it, the Middle-East now too.

Another way all my children to see better, how they do,
outsiders cutting a big slice of your "apple pie" and "taking" it away,
to strangers not right like them and without your permission
was taking a slice of your "mother-land," and nothing you can say!
Black people on this side, couldn't do nothing
good people on their bias bad side, could have done something...but doing nothing, could be just as bad a curse
allowing the next time with no excuses, to become much worst.
History Cleo roared real loud this time, its' called "fool-ya,"
the jungle animals cried out what's that again you say?
History Cleo straining roared louder its' called "fool-ya"
little by little with no respect they'll "sock it to ya."
Black History Month is first "Kemet History" contributions to you,
to be recognized, won't be apologized wrong doings by them
still till today from ancient times what bad they do.
And if all jungle animals could really talk
just imagine what they'd say loud and clear,
just what they saw since ancient history would be
the proud black story, about the world's best "rich" land here,
and until science can recycle animal sounds people can understand
we'll store in our minds the black man's greatness that's dear.
Like from a talking library, I remember being told
my ancestry of lions laid beside thrones of old
heard all goings on of kings and Queens
who ruled with justice, law and order some as a team,
trained to obey and protect their masters with instinct
chained with a spiked collar made them look really mean.
Laid at their feet hearing of invaders, wars, and black defeat...

HA-HE-HA-AU-Hee-Hee

HA-HA

Suddenly giggling and heckling came from "Silly Willy" laughing Hyena,
envious jealous invaders stole the black's joy, last war couldn't compete.
Angry animals shouted, shut-up Silly Willy that
ain't really funny, where you coming from man
from all of us, you need a good kick-in-the-can!
This is not a question of maybe or just guessing,
this is a true love for God's children, Black history lesson.
How a mystery hidden of Black history, must be told
will protect children's minds with adult protection standing bold.

"Sid," the signifying Monkey while swinging jumped from a tree,

squealing monkey ancestry remembered skillful Black Queen Cleopatra,

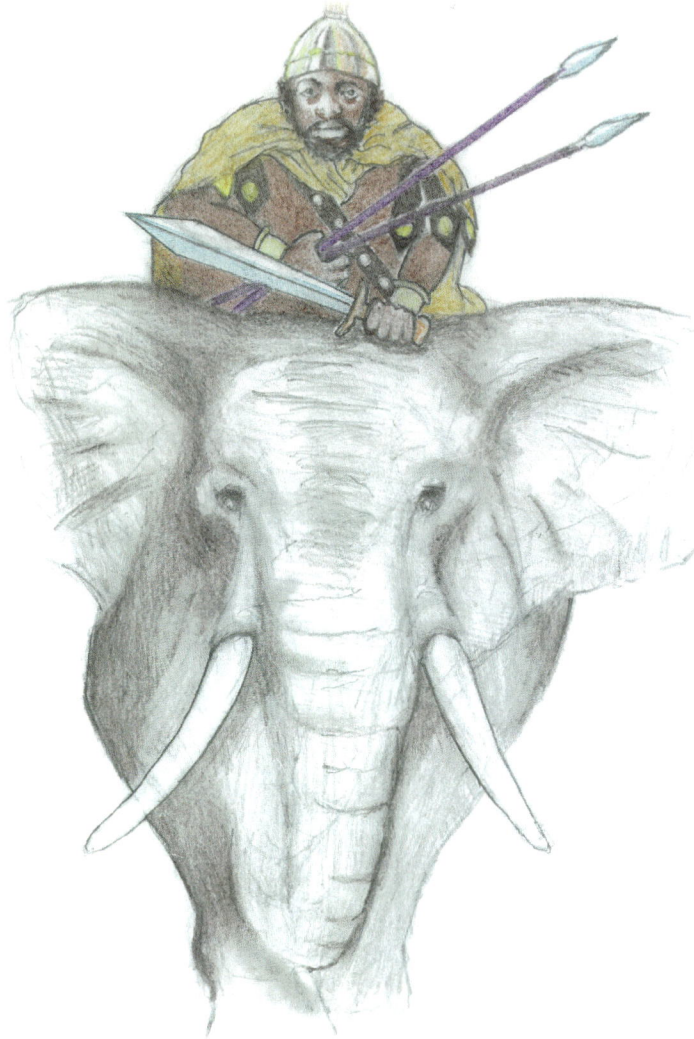

black warrior Hannibal conquering with elephants, was
unbelievable history,
however, today they bleach their color in "Hollywood" is
unanswered mystery.
Again, "Silly Willy" the laughing Hyena giggling loud with
interruption,
don't forget the great pyramids of Giza the blacks designed
and built a wonder of how, is still a mystery of production.

The great "Sphinx" shows a King with a "lion's body,"
was a beware warning at Giza largest statue of stone
guarding temples, palaces jewelry and gold in silence and alone.
Foreigners foolish-pride wrongly chipped away to hide the truth,
the flat nose and thick lips telling through time
identity images showing evidence, for the original Blackman's proof.
Understandings incorrect showing, the pyramids as a white European introduction
has once again a bad smell of Euro-Western renaming, in picture corruption;
because Arabs and Jews were born around 1675 B.C.E.
some 900 years after the greatest pyramid of black people's construction.
Seems a dislike or prejudice against real African history to be known,
Like, the original architect of Giza's colossal pyramids were black to the bone
however, his black picture in front his own creation with respect, is never shown.

African Americans are look-a-like ancient proud Nubians, of the Kemet Nation;
pyramid architect is black-power's greatest wonder, the world to see of his creation,
and for education to all children, correction is rightful justice, progressing civilization.
Euro-Western teachings to blacks, won't explain how great black civilizations flourished,
perhaps envied other lands, their land no-longer could support
conquered with wars, for their over-population they had to feed and nourish.
Ethiopia and Abyssinia Nubians were the Ethiopian ancient Kushite Empire
also was a mixture of the oldest and purest black Arabian blood,
original black Arabians of the Tigris and Euphrates Rivers way-before Noah's flood,
not a few Arabs seemingly white European, the flunky yes-man newcomer, imposters;
overseer of histories and culture nothing completely belong to them made deals
sold-out stolen black Kemet history, art and artifacts to European crooked monsters
and Arab imposters replicate America's black flunky yes-man, called Uncle Tom.
Black Arabia is the Black African prostrating to Allah, "origin of Islam,"
no different than the cross of Christianity or American Indians
praising natures spirits of God sitting cross-legged, in their 'wigwam."
This lesson will enlighten a child, like the unconditional love of a caring mother,
is telling all children of different countries, to be proud of their "skin-color."
A seed grows into a beautiful flower; hard well learned knowledge is power!
This truth of history will set everybody young and old liberated free
will make communicating and understanding so much better,
is a history lesson humble for peaceful co-existing, genuine to every letter.

Then there was "Blake the Snake," hissing his ancestry saw Blacks

gather herbs for "Imhotep" of Kemet, black medicine maker
world's first genius had medicine over 2,000 years, the creator
way before the European Greeks visited and became a taker
 coming to Africa, looking to learn secrets to cure illnesses, they came,
went back to Greece lied "Hippocrates" the father of medicine's fame.

Study children, learn with discipline, create, invent, sell ideas, imagination,
a key for success under God, make it your business
build with ingredients like baking a cake was the "Kemet nation,"
 bonafide making Africa their dear motherland and Blacks the first civilization
Blake the Snake was wide open now and kept hissing on without shame,
said bad white Americans punished slaves, even learning to write their name
did not want the bent into submission "slave" to read or write,
because if he read the Bible, would've knew it was about them
denied Blacks self-esteem; keeping them deaf, dumb, blind and up-tight.
The black church became a refuge but mostly important to learn,
avoiding White hate to harm, church was the safest place to turn.
Goodwill of truth must be said by all means
 like black slaves old-saying, they come from African Kings and Queens
 but having a common touch for foods like black beans and rice,

their common king's name in the Bible was Black Jesus Christ.
The word of God in the Bible teaches and warns
black and all others must pay the price
to walk the straight and narrow right way,

means living by black Moses 10 commandments and need to pray.
You have to tell the truth in history and let it fall where it may,
Biblical prophet Black Moses departed a sea that led the way
that freed his people, snakes over-heard God and Moses say.
A little white lie in pictures seen long enough becomes the truth,
or hoping false teachings twist words they pick
hope said long and hard enough will stick, like
nowhere is it written a White Christ having any evidence of proof.
With no intent to insult or hurt; only giving children truth,
like children with bad health habits causing cavities
given a dentist; a must having to pull, a poison decaying tooth.
History Cleo roared, getting down about the old and the new

"Gary" the Giraffe grunted an old story of his ancestor
while eating leaves looking between the branches of a tree,
reported seeing strangers trap Africa's sons and daughters
hurt, tied them up, and taken away, things that shouldn't be.
Was told later on they stole people, put them in chains
were strange looking men, bad racist bullies who lie and cheat
took them across the Atlantic ocean, not knowing what they'd meet,
and from blood, sweat, and tears built the strongest nation America
the modern world has ever seen, that no other can beat.
For all children to understand truth has to be said
here cartoon animals are giving truth, of what is read,
children's future will create Black History Month's achievements ahead.
"world's first university" in Black land of Mali Africa was called "Timbuktu."
Blacks created arithmetic, algebra, higher mathematics and all the sciences.
There's much more Black History Month next celebration may bring to you,
Like, giving ancient South American Aztec their pyramids and knowledge,
watered ancient American Indians wisdom, that grew their spiritual thirst.
A lot of biblical things people may never know, who even been to college
no matter how its argued, disguised nor how the Bible been bleached,
it's a history book what heights, "original" Black men reached.
And to our Nubian or African American sisters and brothers,
our "Motherland Africa" must start "Black History Month"
as her precious lost sons and daughters.
For all children to understand the truth has to be said,
here cartoon animals explain the truth of what you read,
we animals must settle for surviving in jungles and on open flat range,
but the Blackman's unity "is the power," to make change!
A lie might glitter better, does not change the truth sounding strange.
After hearing what Gary said, the jungle animals cheered with glee
this meeting in February is for the Blackmans history

whose proud black Americans will always honor however,

speaking first of his rich and beautiful Motherland, is missing!

Relate to riches of the simple joys of black folk honest living

learn unity sponsoring for Africa's natural resources, economics knowledge bonding

wealthy black Africans and black Americans together, who control expanding, giving

a new inter-national power base, creating black merchandise businesses, beginning!

The beautiful history of the original Blackman must remain,

with no more bleached changes, kept only by us, to maintain.

This child's short history is not big me and little you,

but only about real things that were done by who,

and who did what and what was really sure enough true;

like the sky sometimes turns dark or light with other colors

but always in the end returns, back to itself sky blue,

now let History Cleo continue next, to "boo-ga-loo."

History Cleo roared, this is a lesson no-one can deny,

bad people who cheat, steal, and lie

can't fool all the people all the time;

is just like saying the great bald eagle can't fly

and breaking hearts catches up with you by and bye,

makes in the end twice as hard, you cry.

Terrible things always happen; who lie, steal, deal corruption or cheat,

we all at one pitiful time or acting grand another...

may weaken and do a little wrong of each.

Have faith in man, only in God we trust

because no one is perfect, even those who teach,

pray and obey the lessons in your church who preach;

and whatever good is in your honest goal, you will surely reach.

Remember besides your mother, be your "own best friend,"

hoping we happily enjoyed this history lesson that we'll "cherish," but

sadly this Black History Month "awareness story good-time," must end.

Lightning Source UK Ltd.
Milton Keynes UK
UKIC02n2309271215
265419UK00011B/77